Evangelistic Praying

Evangelistic Praying

by
John MacArthur, Jr.

WORD OF GRACE COMMUNICATIONS
P.O. Box 4000
Panorama City, CA 91412

All Scripture quotations, unless noted otherwise, are from the *New Scofield
Reference Bible*, King James Version. Copyright © 1967 by Oxford Univer-
sity Press, Inc. Reprinted by permission.

Library of Congress Cataloging in Publication Data

MacArthur, John, 1939-
    Evangelistic praying.

    (John MacArthur Bible studies)
    Bible studies taken from messages delivered at
Grace Community Church in Panorama City, California.
    Includes indexes.
    1. Bible.   N.T.   Timothy, 1st, II, 1-8—Criticism,
interpretation, etc.   2. Bible.   N.T.   Matthew IX, 35-X,
1—Criticism, interpretation, etc.   3. Evangelistic
work—Biblical teaching.   4. Prayer—Biblical teaching.
I. Title.   II. Series: MacArthur, John, 1939-
Bible studies.
BS2745.2.M3   1988   243   88-7200
ISBN   0-8024-5362-7

1 2 3 4 5 6 Printing/LC/Year 92 91 90 89 88

Contents

These Bible studies are taken from messages delivered by Pastor-Teacher John MacArthur, Jr., at Grace Community Church in Panorama City, California. These messages have been combined into a 4-tape album entitled *Evangelistic Praying*. You may purchase this series either in an attractive vinyl cassette album or as individual cassettes. To purchase these tapes, request the album *Evangelistic Praying*, or ask for the tapes by their individual GC numbers. Please consult the current price list; then, send your order, making your check payable to:

WORD OF GRACE COMMUNICATIONS
P.O. Box 4000
Panorama City, CA 91412

Or call the following toll-free number:
1-800-55-GRACE

Pray that enemy from... interfering in the work of Harvest 88 in

1
Evangelistic Praying—Part 1

Outline

Introduction
A. Examples of Praying for the Lost
   1. In the Old Testament
      a) Moses
      b) Samuel
      c) Jeremiah
      d) Hezekiah
      e) Daniel
   2. In the New Testament
      a) Stephen
      b) Paul
B. Reluctance Toward Praying for the Lost
   1. Identified as exclusiveness
   2. Illustrated by Israel
C. The Importance of Praying for the Lost
   1. It is an exhortation
   2. It is the church's primary objective

Lesson
 I. The Nature of Evangelistic Praying (v. 1*b*)
    A. Praying with a Sense of Need
    B. Praying to Honor God
    C. Praying Out of Concern for Others
    D. Praying with a Thankful Heart
II. The Scope of Evangelistic Praying (vv. 1*c*-2*a*)
    A. Outlined (v. 1*c*)
    B. Applied (v. 2*a*)

1. A neglected group
2. An ignored directive
3. An unexpected result

Conclusion

Introduction

Some years ago I was given a book on prayer written by a reputable Christian author. It concluded that the Bible does not command us to pray for the lost but for laborers to reach the lost. He cited Matthew 9:38, where the Lord tells His disciples to "pray . . . that he will send forth laborers into his harvest." The book's thesis was that we are called to evangelize. However, the author also concluded that praying for the lost was relatively unimportant. Once we justify not praying for the lost, it becomes easy to neglect that important dimension of our spiritual lives, because fervent evangelistic prayer takes time and energy. The Holy Spirit used 1 Timothy 2:1-8 to remind me of the importance of evangelistic praying.

Praying for the lost is part of our lives. When someone we love doesn't know Christ, it's natural to pray for his conversion. First Timothy 2:1-8, however, is not only a command to pray for those we love who are lost, but it is an expression of the scope of evangelistic praying. It compels us to pray on a wider scale than perhaps we have previously understood. We need to know what the Bible teaches about such prayer. Is it legitimate? Is it necessary? Can we really pray for the salvation of a person? Of a city? Of a state? Of a nation? Does praying in such broad terms have any significance in the mind of God?

A. Examples of Praying for the Lost

1. In the Old Testament

   a) Moses

   In Numbers 11:1-2 Moses prays for God not to consume the unbelieving, complaining Israelites in fiery judgment. In 14:19 he cries out to God, saying, "Pardon, I beseech thee, the iniquity of this people according unto the greatness of thy mercy." Moses, a man of God and the leader of Israel, expressed to God his heart's burning desire for Israel's salvation. That is evangelistic praying.

b) Samuel

In 1 Samuel 12:23-25 Samuel says to the Israelites, "As for me, God forbid that I should sin against the Lord in ceasing to pray for you; but I will teach you the good and the right way. Only fear the Lord, and serve him in truth with all your heart; for consider how great things he hath done for you. But if ye shall still do wickedly, ye shall be consumed, both ye and your king." Samuel was saying not only that his praying for the Israelites was important, but that it was sin not to pray. If Samuel had failed to pray that his people would fear the Lord and serve Him, they would have been consumed in their wickedness. His prayer was for the conversion of unredeemed Israelites. In 1 Samuel 7 Samuel calls idolatrous Israel to return to the Lord and put away her idols (v. 3). When the Israelites obeyed, he called them to gather at Mizpah for what was to be a great evangelistic meeting. And he said to them, "I will pray for you" (v. 5). He was saying he would pray that God would be merciful and forgive their sin.

c) Jeremiah

God, after speaking to the Israelites about their wickedness, said, "Because ye have done all these works . . . and I spoke unto you, rising up early and speaking, but ye heard not; and I called you, but ye answered not; therefore will I do unto this house, which is called by my name, in which ye trust, and unto the place which I gave to you and to your fathers, as I have done to Shiloh. And I will cast you out of my sight, as I have cast out all your brethren, even the whole seed of Ephraim. Therefore, pray not for this people, neither lift up cry nor prayer for them, neither make intercession to me; for I will not hear thee" (Jer. 7:13-16). From the testimony of Jeremiah, we know that a major part of his ministry was crying to God on behalf of His people. Jeremiah wept

9

bitterly and cried out to God that Israel would be brought to faith in Him. But the Israelites had continued in sin so long that God told Jeremiah to stop praying for them.

In Jeremiah 14:10-13 Jeremiah says, "Thus saith the Lord unto this people, Thus have they loved to wander, they have not restrained their feet; therefore, the Lord doth not accept them; he will now remember their iniquity, and punish their sins. Then said the Lord unto me, Pray not for this people for their good. When they fast, I will not hear their cry, and when they offer burnt offering and an oblation, I will not accept them; but I will consume them by the sword, and by the famine, and by the pestilence. Then said I, Ah, Lord God!" Jeremiah was determined to pray for his people: only God could stop him.

d) Hezekiah

Hezekiah, king of Judah, observed his people gathering in Jerusalem for the Passover. He noted many had not properly cleansed themselves (2 Chron. 30:17-18). They were an impure people, practicing an external and hypocritical religion. Hezekiah prayed, "The good Lord pardon everyone who prepareth his heart to seek God" (vv. 18-19). Hezekiah was praying for the salvation of his people.

e) Daniel

In Daniel 9:17-19 Daniel prays, "Now, therefore, O our God, hear the prayer of thy servant, and his supplications, and cause thy face to shine upon thy sanctuary that is desolate, for the Lord's sake. O my God, incline thine ear, and hear; open thine eyes, and behold our desolations, and the city which is called by thy name; for we do not present our supplications before thee for our righteousnesses, but for thy great mercies. O Lord, hear; O Lord, forgive; O Lord, hearken and do; defer not, for thine own sake, O my God; for thy city and thy people are called by thy name." Daniel entreated God to forgive His sinful people and restore them, their city, and their worship.

2. In the New Testament

a) Stephen

Stephen was stoned to death for what the Jewish people saw as blasphemy—the gospel of Christ. As he was being stoned, he asked the Lord to receive him, and then he prayed this marvelous prayer: "Lord, lay not this sin to their charge" (Acts 7:60), which is to say, "O God, be merciful to these sinners." He prayed for their forgiveness and salvation.

b) Paul

In Romans 9:2 Paul says he has "great heaviness and continual sorrow in [his] heart." In verse 3 he explains: "I could wish that I myself were accursed from Christ for my brethren [the Jewish people], my kinsmen according to the flesh." In 10:1 he says, "My heart's desire and prayer to God for Israel is, that they might be saved."

Praying for those who aren't saved is clearly a biblical principle. Paul gives a full explanation of that kind of praying in 1 Timothy 2.

B. Reluctance Toward Praying for the Lost

First Timothy 2:1-8 is a polemic. Something is wrong in the church, and those verses are intended to set it right. There are three primary propositions in those eight verses: Christians should pray for the salvation of all people (v. 1), God wants all people to be saved (v. 4), and believers must meet certain conditions to pray acceptably (v. 8). Those conditions are godly behavior ("holy hands") and pure inward motivation ("without wrath and doubting").

The main point of the passage is that the church is called to pray for the lost on a wide scale. It may be that the church at Ephesus was not committed to praying for all people, or not committed to the truth that God wants all people saved. When they did pray, they may have been praying with soiled hands and angry, dissenting hearts.

1. Identified as exclusiveness

   In the church at Ephesus there was a Judaizing element that claimed God would save only those who kept the Mosaic law (1 Tim. 1:7-11). The result was an exclusiveness that limited salvation to those who kept the law.

   Some Gentiles in the church had also developed an exclusiveness that was rooted in a philosophy that later developed into gnosticism. They believed salvation belonged only to elite, initiated people who reached a certain level of knowledge (6:20-21). They believed they had mystical experiences with various sub-gods and angelic beings, which Paul identified as demons (4:1).

   Because of such exclusiveness, members of the Ephesian church made a severe error concerning the doctrine of salvation. Paul concluded the epistle by saying that some had "erred concerning the faith" (1 Tim. 6:21). Their greatest error concerned the extent of salvation. Some said only those who kept the law could be saved; others said God reserved salvation for those who reached a particular level of knowledge. Everyone else was left out.

   First Timothy 2:1-8 attacks that narrow perspective. Paul wanted the church to realize that God desires all people to be saved. The Ephesian heresies shared the belief that not all people are fit subjects for salvation, neither are all people the objects of God's desire. Paul counteracted their exclusiveness by showing their need to pray for all people to be saved.

2. Illustrated by Israel

   As a Jew, Paul knew Jewish history well. One glaring failure that tarnished Israel's history was not recognizing the universality of her mission. The Israelites lived under the illusion that God saved them for their own sake and not the world's. They thought of themselves as a bucket rather than a channel. Because God had saved them and made them His special people, they believed they should keep Gentiles from sharing their unique position.

The book of Jonah is a graphic illustration of Israel's mentality. God called Jonah to go to Nineveh and preach to Gentiles (1:2). Being Jewish, however, Jonah couldn't tolerate a Gentile coming into favor with God, so he fled to Nineveh (1:3). Some commentators maintain that Jonah fled because of fear or feelings of inadequacy. But chapter 4 implies he fled because he didn't want Gentiles sharing the exclusive blessing of God that Israel believed she alone deserved. After the great fish vomited him up on the shore (2:10), he went to Nineveh and preached (3:3-4). And something terrible happened—the entire city repented (3:5-9)! Then Jonah asked God to take his life (4:3) because his worst fears had come to pass: Gentiles had been saved. What a pathetic attitude!

The sad truth of redemptive history is that Israel failed to be a channel for God to reach the world. When God saw that channel blocked by sin and selfishness, He chose a new one—the church, a redeemed community from all nations that was God's witnessing community. Paul didn't want the mentality that destroyed Israel's effectiveness to form in the Ephesian congregation. Therefore he instructed them about the need for evangelistic prayer that was worldwide in its scope.

C. The Importance of Praying for the Lost

1. It is an exhortation

Paul begins chapter 2 by saying, "I exhort." He could have commanded them, but instead he uses a word that refers to begging, beseeching, or urging because of a sense of urgency. A command bears authority; an exhortation bears passion. A command comes from a king, an exhortation from a loved one. Paul came as a passionate apostle, knowing that prayer isn't forced by a command but prompted by the heart.

The Greek word translated "therefore" in verse 1 tells us Paul's exhortation is based on what he said: that Timothy had been given a divine commission to stand up for the faith.

2. It is the church's primary objective

Paul stressed the priority of evangelistic praying by saying "first of all." Praying for the lost is important because it is intimately related to the church's primary objective. The church must remember why it is in the world. If our primary objective were fellowship, we would be in heaven where we would enjoy perfect fellowship. If our primary objective were knowledge of God's Word, we would be in heaven, where our knowledge will be complete. The church is in the world to reach the lost. But if the church entertains a theology that limits the scope of the gospel, that priority will be ignored. We as believers must realize that God desires all people to be saved and that we, therefore, are called to pray with holy hands and a pure heart for all people.

Lesson

I. THE NATURE OF EVANGELISTIC PRAYING (v. 1*b*)

"Supplications, prayers, intercessions, and giving of thanks."

These are four words that could be used interchangeably for the word *prayer*. Since the Holy Spirit inspired Paul to use four similar terms, He must intend for us to examine them and see shades of variation, which brings richness to the concept of prayer.

A. Praying with a Sense of Need

"Supplications."

The Greek word translated "supplications" (*deēsis*) occurs often in Scripture. It comes from a verb root that refers to lacking or being deprived of something. Supplication therefore speaks of prayer that rises from a sense of need. When someone is without something he desperately needs, he goes where he can receive it. Evangelistic praying springs from a sense of need.

We understand that those who are without Christ desperately need Him. We are fully aware that those who don't know the Savior and don't have forgiveness of sin are heading toward an eternity without God in hell. Supplication responds to a need, and when we look realistically and scripturally at our lost world, we realize the graveness of its need. It also implies approaching someone who has the resources to supply the need. If we want to understand the nature of evangelistic praying, we must begin by realizing the great need of the lost in the world.

B. Praying to Honor God

"Prayers."

The Greek word translated "prayers" (*proseuchē*) is a general word for prayer addressed only to God. It seems to connote worship and reverence. We pray for lost souls to come to salvation not only because of their great need but also because of God's great glory. Our overwhelming interest must be that God might be exalted, glorified, and praised. In John 14 Jesus says that the ultimate goal of everything we pray is "that the Father may be glorified in the Son" (v. 13). We pray for the salvation of others because God is so worthy of praise, glory, adoration, and honor that it is an offense against His Person for any creature not to give Him what He is due.

C. Praying Out of Concern for Others

"Intercessions."

"Intercessions" (Gk., *enteuxis*), used only here and in 1 Timothy 4:5, suggests praying on behalf of someone else. The verb form of the Greek word means "to fall in with a person," "to become intimately involved with someone," or "to converse with familiarity." We are not interceding for people as if we were some cold, legal attorney or advocate.

Christ, Our Intimate Advocate

Usually when we think of the Lord Jesus Christ as our advocate (Heb. 7:25), we conjure up images of a powdered wig, a legal robe, and a courtroom where Christ is our attorney. When we think of the Holy Spirit's interceding for us (Rom. 8:26), we think of a legal transaction. But the Greek word suggests much more than that. In Hebrews 7:25 and Romans 8:26 the richness of the word denotes that Christ and the Holy Spirit are so near to us that we can converse with them as with friends. They become involved in our struggles. *Enteuxis* is not only a word of advocacy but also of empathy, compassion, and involvement.

To intercede for others is not to coldly request the salvation of those we care little about. It is to sympathetically enter into the depth of their anxiety and pain and to cry out to God on their behalf. We need to be compassionately involved in the problems of the lost.

I am convinced that our praying tends to be shallow and impotent because we don't live with a sobering awareness of man's need and the desperate state of the lost. Neither do we live with an all-consuming desire to see God glorified in the salvation of souls. We tend to be so self-centered that we avoid getting involved in the lives of those who need our prayers.

D. Praying with a Thankful Heart

"Giving of thanks."

We should thank God for the privilege of reaching others with the good news of Jesus Christ. Since we believe anyone can be saved, we can thank God that the gospel is extended to all. Regardless of the answers to our prayers, we can be thankful to God. First Thessalonians 5:18 says, "In everything give thanks; for this is the will of God in Christ Jesus concerning you." Because thanksgiving is the only element of prayer that will continue after we've entered His presence for eternity, it should be part of the prayers we offer here.

...onfined to our personal in-
...nally extend to an unsaved
...aul's point is that we should
...stic praying is universal in
...ss, no special group, no elite.
...initiates who alone can come
... to pray for all of the unre-
...that by saying God wants "all
...adds that Christ "gave himself a

...o have that scope because God
...verywhere to repent" (Acts 17:30).
...hy 2 any limitation is foreign to the
...the context. Because all people ev-
...nded to repent, we must pray they
...ce of God that bringeth salvation" (Titus 2:11). ... "Go ye into all the world, and preach
the gospel to every creature" (Mark 16:15). Christ died for
all people, so all people are savable in that sense, and we
should pray for them. Praying for the lost should be a con-
stant and integral part of the church.

B. Applied (v. 2a)

"For kings, and for all that are in authority."

1. A neglected group

Paul identifies one special category of people the church
is to pray for: the authorities. Perhaps he isolates that
group because the tendency of the church is not to pray
for them. Sometimes leaders are abusive, generating ha-
tred and bitterness. At other times they seem larger
than life, and the church feels little responsibility to pray
for them because they don't know them. But they play a
tremendous role in the church's ability to "lead a tran-

quil and quiet life in all godliness and dignity" (v. 2*b*, NASB*). In any society the government establishes the boundaries of the church's function and freedom. Because they have that authority, we ought to pray for our leaders.

There may have been a tendency among Ephesian Christians to speak evil of their authorities. The Greek noun translated "king" (*basileus*) can be translated "emperor" and probably should be here. When Paul wrote 1 Timothy, the emperor of Rome was Nero, a wicked, perverted man who persecuted Christians. We can understand why the church wasn't excited about praying for him. But Paul specifically mentioned praying for the emperor—and "for *all* that are in authority" (emphasis added). We should pray for all who are in authority in any generation, whether emperors or procurators, senators or town clerks.

2. An ignored directive

Perhaps most Christians have prayed that their leaders will be wise and will do what's right. But the text exhorts us to pray for their salvation. God wants all people to be saved so that His truth can be operative in society. So pray for the salvation of all leaders, whether they're good or bad, beneficent or cruel, peaceful or warlike. Notice Paul didn't say to pray that God will remove those who disagree with you. And he certainly didn't say to ask God to replace them with Christians. Instead he said to pray that God will save them.

Is Christianity Political Activism?

Romans 13:1-7 teaches that believers should be loyal to the government because it is ordained of God. First Peter 2:13-17 says we should be respectful and obedient to government so that nothing can be said against us. Christians are to be a model of loyalty. Although 1 Timothy 2 clearly teaches us to pray for our leaders, many evangelical Christians attack them instead. It would be wonderful if the church used the energy it spends in political maneuvering

**New American Standard Bible.*

18

our weapons though

and lobbying to pray for the salvation of its leaders. Can you imagine the impact on our leaders if they knew all Christians were praying daily for their salvation? What a way to activate the power of God! We have forgotten that the weapons of our warfare are not fleshly. Why does the church emasculate itself by using carnal methods? Our weapons are spiritual and "mighty through God to the pulling down of [Satan's] strongholds" (2 Cor. 10:4). The way to change a nation is through prayer (cf. 2 Chron. 10:4). But instead of praying, too often we speak evil of those we disagree with and create Christian power groups to replace them. In so doing we become the enemy and pollute for them the water of life. The church must always use spiritual weapons—never worldly ones.

GOD ↑

3. An unexpected result

Does God answer our prayer for the salvation of others? As Stephen was being stoned to death, he prayed for the salvation of those who stoned him. Could it be that the salvation of one standing among those killers was the result of his prayer? It's possible that Paul's salvation was the answer to Stephen's simple, sincere prayer.

Paul and Silas had been beaten, bound in stocks, and thrown in jail in the city of Philippi. Acts 16:25 says that while they were there, they were singing and praying. Could it be they were praying for the salvation of the one in authority over them—the jailer? In His marvelous providence God may have arranged the earthquake and the other circumstances so the Philippian jailer and his whole household would be redeemed that night in answer to the prayer of Paul and Silas.

Conclusion

In Acts 26 Paul makes his defense before Agrippa. After Paul asked him if he believed the prophets (v. 27), Agrippa accused Paul of trying to persuade him to become a Christian (v. 28). Paul replied, "I would to God that not only thou but also all that hear me this day were both almost, and altogether, such as I am, except these bonds" (v. 29). Basically he was saying he wanted everyone in the

19

room to be saved. Evangelistic praying was the heartbeat of the apostle Paul and must be a priority of the church.

We cultivate the spirit of evangelistic prayer by sensing the need of those who are lost and damned to hell, and having as our primary desire the glory and honor of God. Nineteenth-century English missionary Henry Martyn reflected such an attitude. When he saw pagans worshiping in India he said he could not endure existence if Jesus was to be so dishonored. Evangelistic prayer also expresses itself in our becoming so pained over the state of the lost that we cry out to God for them. Nevertheless we remain thankful to God for whatever He does in His sovereign wisdom. The scope of evangelistic praying is for all people, especially those who rule over us.

The story is told of a little girl in Sunday school who was deaf and dumb. As part of the lesson, the teacher wrote on a piece of paper: "What is prayer?" The little girl wrote: "Prayer is the wish of the heart." She's right. That's what prayer is, whether it finds its way to the lips or not. Is the wish of your heart that all people would be saved? If it is, that wish will rise to God.

Focusing on the Facts

1. What does 1 Timothy 2:1-8 command us to do (see p. 8)?
2. Explain what Samuel, Jeremiah, and Paul teach us about praying for the lost (see pp. 9-11).
3. What problems in the church at Ephesus was 1 Timothy 2:1-8 written to correct (see p. 11)?
4. Explain the nature of the Jewish and Gentile exclusiveness in Ephesus (see p. 12).
5. What doctrine did their exclusiveness affect? Explain (see p. 12).
6. What glaring failure tarnished Israel's history? What Old Testament prophet illustrates that? Explain (see pp. 12-13).
7. What is the difference between a command and an exhortation? Why did Paul use an exhortation in 1 Timothy 2 (see p. 13)?
8. Why is the church in the world (see p. 14)?
9. What four words does Paul use to express the nature of prayer? Explain the significance of each (1 Tim. 2:1; see pp. 14-16).
10. What should be the ultimate goal of everything we pray (John 14:13; see p. 15)?

11. Why should we pray for all people (see p. 17)?
12. Praying for the lost should be a _____ and _____ part of the church (see p. 17).
13. Why does Paul single out those in authority as ones we should pray for (see p. 17)?
14. What insight does 1 Timothy 2:2 reveal about why we should pray for our leaders? What should we pray for them (see pp. 17-18)?
15. Explain what 2 Corinthians 10:4 leads us to conclude about political activism in the church (see p. 19).

Pondering the Principles

1. In the Ephesian church some believers limited the scope of the gospel by developing an exclusive mind-set. Today some Christians limit the gospel's scope by nurturing some learned prejudice against a particular group. Do any racial or cultural prejudices cause you to snub certain people and be less concerned about their salvation? Ask God to forgive you and to give you the kind of love for others that Christ had, regardless of the color of their skin or the clothes they wear. Memorize 1 Timothy 2:3-4, and begin to pray for and befriend someone in the group you had snubbed.

2. Read about the nature of evangelistic praying on pages 14-16. How does your praying for the lost compare with the biblical exhortation? Read the following passages to increase your sensitivity to each aspect:

   • Praying with a sense of need (Rom. 3:10-19; Rev. 20:11-15)
   • Praying to honor God (John 14:13; 1 Cor. 10:31; Rev. 5:11-14)
   • Praying out of concern for others (Matt. 23:37; Rom. 9:1-5)
   • Praying with a thankful heart (Phil. 4:6-7; 1 Thess. 1:2-3)

2
Evangelistic Praying—Part 2

Outline

Introduction

Review
  I. The Nature of Evangelistic Praying (v. 1b)
 II. The Scope of Evangelistic Praying (vv. 1c-2a)

Lesson
III. The Benefit of Evangelistic Praying (v. 2b)
   A. Its Characteristics
      1. An absence of disturbance
      2. An atmosphere for growth
         a) Through a reverent attitude
         b) Through right actions
   B. Its Apparent Contradictions
      1. Godliness creates disturbances
      2. Suffering perfects faith
 IV. The Reasons for Evangelistic Praying (vv. 3-7)
   A. It Is Morally Right (v. 3a)
      1. An obvious point
      2. An apparent objection
         a) Confusion over John 17:9
         b) Clarification of John 17:9
   B. It Is God's Will (vv. 3b-4)
      1. Because of His character (v. 3b)
      2. Because of His desire (v. 4)
         a) Illustrating His desire
            (1) In the Old Testament
               (a) The book of Isaiah
               (b) The book of Ezekiel
            (2) In the New Testament

b) Explaining His desire
    (1) God wants everyone to be saved
    (2) Not everyone will be saved

Introduction

Because the theme of 1 Timothy 2:1-8 is evangelistic praying, I decided to read some books about evangelism. One was a compilation of sermons by nineteenth-century English preacher Charles Haddon Spurgeon called *The Soul Winner*. One paragraph that struck my heart said:

"The soul-winner must be a master of the art of prayer. You cannot bring souls to God if you do not go to God yourself. You must get your battle-axe, and your weapons of war, from the armoury of sacred communication with Christ. If you are much alone with Jesus, you will catch His Spirit. You will be fired with the flame that burned in His breast and consumed His life. You will weep with the tears that fell upon Jerusalem when He saw it perishing; and if you cannot speak so eloquently as He did, yet shall there be about what you say somewhat of the same power which in Him thrilled the hearts and awoke the consciences of men. My dear hearers, especially you members of the church, I am always so anxious lest any of you should begin to lie upon your oars, and take things easy in the matters of God's Kingdom. There are some of you—I bless you, and I bless God at the remembrance of you—who are in season, and out of season, in earnest for winning souls, and you are the truly wise; but I fear there are others whose hands are slack, who are satisfied to let me preach, but do not themselves preach; who take these seats, and occupy these pews, and hope the cause goes well, but that is all they do" ([Grand Rapids: Eerdmans, 1963], pp. 246-47).

Every true-hearted pastor can identify with Spurgeon, because the apathy that characterized some of the people in his church is present in the church today. Apathy stifles aggressive witnessing and evangelistic praying. We need to be reminded to reach the lost, and an essential element in reaching them is praying for them.

Timothy had been assigned to set things in order in a church that had many problems. One problem was that some members of the Ephesian church had designed a new theology of evangelism that limited salvation either to Jews who kept the law or to elite Gentiles who understood certain mystical secrets. Because of his deep concern, Paul wrote Timothy to correct those errors. He began by reminding the Ephesian Christians that God desires all people to come to a saving knowledge of the Lord Jesus Christ. Therefore, one of the church's highest priorities is to pray for the lost.

High Priorities

I. THE NATURE OF EVANGELISTIC PRAYING (v. 1b; see pp. 14-16)

"Supplications, prayers, intercessions, and giving of thanks."

In 1 Timothy 2:1 Paul defines the nature of evangelistic praying in four ways: "supplications, prayers, intercessions, and giving of thanks." The Greek word translated "supplications" indicates we should pray for the lost because of their great need for salvation. The Greek word for "prayers" teaches us to pray for the salvation of others because of the glory it will give to God. The Greek word for "intercessions" reveals we should compassionately empathize with the lost. And "giving of thanks" indicates that regardless of what occurs, we should thank God for the opportunity to tell others about Christ.

II. THE SCOPE OF EVANGELISTIC PRAYING (vv. 1c-2a; see pp. 17-20)

"Be made for all men, for kings, and for all that are in authority."

Paul gives a comprehensive mandate to the church to pray for all people. Within that category he specifies a group that the church might neglect—all those in authority. We tend not to pray for our secular leaders because they're bigger than life, antagonistic, or disliked by our society. Our request should be for their salvation (vv. 3-4).

III. THE BENEFIT OF EVANGELISTIC PRAYING (v. 2b)

"That we may lead a quiet and peaceable life in all godliness and honesty."

A. Its Characteristics

When the church in a city, state, or nation prays unceasingly and habitually for the lost, particularly those in its government, people will begin to see the church as compassionate, loving people who seek the interest and welfare of others. As those prayers are answered, the condition of the church becomes more favorable, thus expediting our evangelistic efforts.

1. An absence of disturbance

"A quiet and peaceable life."

The Greek word translated "quiet" (ēremos) speaks of an absence of outside disturbance; "peaceable" (Gk., hēsuchios) of an absence of inside disturbance. The church is to pray with love and compassion for the lost so that it faces no external or internal disturbances. Peace and rest help the church to evangelize. First Thessalonians 4 says, "Make it your ambition to lead a quiet life and attend to your own business and work with your hands . . . so that you may behave properly toward outsiders [unbelievers]" (vv. 11-12, NASB). Christians should be known for their quiet demeanor. We must never attempt to disrupt society by creating disturbances. Unbelievers ought to see us as quiet, diligent, and faithful people. In 2 Thessalonians 3:11-12 Paul says, "We hear that there are some who walk among you disorderly, working not at all but are busybodies. Now them that are such we command and exhort, by our Lord Jesus Christ, that with quietness they work, and eat their own bread."

The church is never to be a political agitator and perceived as an enemy to national security or peace. When someone is reared in a distinctly Christian environment, sometimes he grows not only to hate the evil world's system but also to view everyone in it as an enemy. He becomes bitter against those who deny what he knows is right. However, regardless of the political or philosophical viewpoint of those around us, we must seek to be their friends by praying for them rather than be their enemies by hating and rejecting them.

Being Model Citizens

Christians should be model citizens. That in no way implies we're to be indifferent, apathetic, or without any opinions on secular matters. It does mean we're to be a blessing to all who know us. Unbelievers shouldn't think of the church as a political lobby or wealthy, strong-arm organization that manipulates others to accomplish its selfish purposes. Instead they should think of us as quiet, peace-loving people who submit to the authorities over us and who pray constantly for the salvation of others. If we as the church covenant together to pray for the lost, including our leaders, and refused to engage in power politics, we wouldn't be accused—or even suspected—of disloyalty. Our leaders would be less likely to misconstrue the purpose of our existence and more likely to allow us to worship and evangelize without restriction. We could therefore live quiet and tranquil lives.

2. An atmosphere for growth

"In all godliness and honesty."

a) Through a reverent attitude

The Greek word translated "godliness" (*eusebeia*) occurs often in the pastoral epistles. It speaks of an attitude of reverence. Our reverence for God should characterize our lives, revealing that we live for the majesty, love, holiness, and glory of God. When someone hears the word *Christian*, he ought to think of a person who loves God.

b) Through right actions

The Greek word translated "honesty" (*semnotēs*) is used two other times in the New Testament—in 1 Timothy 3:4 and Titus 2:7. A basic translation is "moral earnestness," which goes beyond a right attitude to include right behavior. An attitude of godliness expresses itself by a commitment to moral living. When holy attitudes and actions characterize our lives, we contribute to the peace and tranquillity of society.

B. Its Apparent Contradictions

1. Godliness creates disturbances

At this point you may be wondering if 1 Timothy 2:2 contradicts other portions of Scripture. After all, doesn't the Bible teach that godliness brings about persecution from sinful people? Won't the rejection of our message eliminate a quiet and tranquil life in some ways? Paul said he was a prisoner because of his testimony (2 Tim. 1:8). In 3:12 he adds, "*All* that will live godly in Christ Jesus shall suffer persecution" (emphasis added). The point is this: if we suffer persecution and bear the resentment and animosity of society, the reason should be that our attitude and behavior is holy, not that we are disruptive and appear to be an enemy. We should live so that others do not perceive us as a threat to the peace and tranquillity of our nation or town. Christians are to be perceived as dignified, morally committed, trustworthy people. By living that way we prevent anyone from speaking evil of the Word of God or God Himself.

Jesus Himself was a friend of sinners (Luke 7:34), and we ought to pray for the lost, especially our leaders, whether we agree with their life-style, morality, and decisions or not. If we disagree, let's disagree because of God's truth and not because of our political or philosophical views. Christians need to understand that if this nation turns to God, it will be by our using spiritual weapons, not carnal ones. Spiritual weapons, such as prayer for the lost, are "mighty through God to the pulling down of strongholds" (2 Cor. 10:4). That kind of

28

prayer results in the conversion of the lost and gives the church a reputation of loyalty, honesty, integrity, and dignity in the community. When believers display holy attitudes and behavior, we are seen not as a threat to society but a benefit to it. That will create a peace and tranquillity that allows evangelism to flourish.

2. Suffering perfects faith

Someone may say, "Doesn't James 1:3-4 say that the *trying* of our faith has a perfecting work?" That is true, but God can try and strengthen us without using hostility from our society that we bring upon ourselves. If God wants someone in the crucible of suffering, He can accomplish that in many different ways; neither the church nor an individual needs to purposely create trouble.

Sometimes God will use persecution as a trial. But if persecution comes, let it come because of what we believe about the Word of God and not because of our own sin (1 Pet. 2:20). In Matthew 5:43-44 Christ tells us how to respond when persecution comes: "Ye have heard that it hath been said, Thou shalt love thy neighbor, and hate thine enemy; but I say unto you, Love your enemies, bless them that curse you, do good to them that hate you, and pray for them who despitefully use you, and persecute you." While Stephen was beneath the stones that were crushing out his life, like so many martyrs throughout church history he cried out, "Lord, lay not this sin to their charge" (Acts 7:60). That is the spirit of Jesus, who on behalf of those who crucified Him said, "Father, forgive them; for they know not what they do" (Luke 23:34).

Conflict may occur, but not because Christians become enemies of the lost. It should occur only because of what we live for and believe. Our society ought to see us as friends—as compassionate, loving people who continually pray for their salvation. Instead of (or in addition to) writing to your congressman to complain, write to tell him you're praying for his salvation and present him with the gospel. I believe God will answer

29

that prayer when we are concerned enough to pray it. People who insist that no nation can ever be godly, that the church can never flourish, and that to accomplish God's work we must attack everyone we don't like deeply concern me. Often someone will ask why I don't preach on political issues. My answer is that I'll attack sin, but I won't go beyond what the Bible says and preach my political or philosophical preferences. People need Christ, and I don't want to alienate them unnecessarily. I don't want anyone to reject Christ because he rejects my personal views. God says to pray for them. When we do, we'll create an environment in which Christianity can flourish.

IV. THE REASONS FOR EVANGELISTIC PRAYING (vv. 3-7)

"For this is good and acceptable in the sight of God, our Savior, who will have all men to be saved, and to come unto the knowledge of the truth. For there is one God, and one mediator between God and men, the man, Christ Jesus, who gave himself a ransom for all, to be testified in due time. For this I am ordained a preacher, and an apostle (I speak the truth in Christ, and lie not), a teacher of the Gentiles [nations] in faith and verity."

A. It Is Morally Right (v. 3a)

"For this is good."

1. An obvious point

The Greek word translated "good" (*kalon*) speaks of something that is intrinsically or morally good. "This" refers to praying for all people, especially our leaders. God says that praying for lost people is morally right. If I asked you if you should pray for the lost, all that is right and good in you would say yes. You understand that salvation delivers people from hell and allows them to glorify God and to have purpose in life and eternity. It frees them to reach others. Since the salvation of others would be the greatest benefit to them, to God, and to everyone else, praying for them is good.

2. An apparent objection

a) Confusion over John 17:9

Someone may consider John 17:9 as an objection to the rightness of such praying and ask, If it's so right, why did Jesus in His high-priestly prayer say, "I pray for them [i.e., the disciples]; I pray not for the world, but for them whom thou hast given me; for they are thine"? At first glance that verse seems to raise doubt about the moral virtue of evangelistic prayer because Christ said He didn't pray for the world.

Does Christ's statement mean God doesn't love the world? Obviously not. John 3:16 says, "God so loved the world, that he gave his only begotten Son," making the point that God gave His Son to fulfill His love for the whole world. Therefore the whole world must be able to receive His gift. First John 2:2 says, "He is the propitiation [the satisfaction of God's wrath] for our sins, and not for ours only, but also for the sins of the whole world." God loves the whole world, He provided a Savior for the whole world, and Christ's sacrifice is capable of turning aside God's wrath against the sins of the whole world. Since Jesus' mission is to the world, why did He say He didn't pray for the world?

b) Clarification of John 17:9

In John 17:21 Christ says, "[I pray] that they all may be one, as thou, Father, art in me, and I in thee, that they also may be one in us; that the world may believe that thou hast sent me." In that verse He actually prayed for the salvation of the world. In verse 23 He says, "I in them, and thou in me, that they may be made perfect in one; and that the world may know that thou hast sent me, and hast loved them, as thou hast loved me." In verse 21 He prays that the world might believe, and in verse 23 that they might know the truth.

Christ meant He wouldn't pray that the world—the *cosmos*, the evil, satanic system—would succeed. He

31

prayed for the disciples to succeed in winning the world, not for the world to succeed in stopping them. He couldn't pray for the world to succeed because it was set against Him. But He could pray for the world's salvation, that it would no longer be evil. He prayed for His disciples to be protected from the world and its ruler, Satan (v. 15), so that they could reach the world (vv. 21, 23).

B. It Is God's Will (vv. 3*b*-4)

"This is . . . acceptable in the sight of God, our Savior, who will have all men to be saved, and to come unto the knowledge of the truth."

The Greek word translated "acceptable" is not *dechomai*, which means "to receive," but *apodechomai*, which refers to gladly receiving, accepting with satisfaction, and welcoming heartily. It's a warm word expressing that the Lord gladly and eagerly responds to our prayers for the world to be saved. That is what He wants.

1. Because of His character (v. 3*b*)

"God, our Savior."

God accepts such prayer heartily because it is consistent with His character. In 1 Timothy 1:1 Paul says he is an apostle of Christ "by the commandment of God, our Savior." In 4:10 he says God "is the Savior of all men." First Thessalonians 5:9 says, "God hath not appointed us to wrath but to obtain salvation by our Lord Jesus Christ." In Titus 1:3 Paul asserts that the ministry of the Word was committed to him "according to the commandment of God, our Savior." Titus 2:10 speaks of "the doctrine of God, our Savior." Titus 3:4 refers to "the kindness and love of God, our Savior." The Bible repeatedly speaks of God as Savior because that is essential to His nature. He is Savior just as He is Creator and Sustainer.

Even to Old Testament saints God revealed Himself as Savior. In 2 Samuel 22:3 David says, "He is my shield, and the horn of my salvation, my high tower, and my refuge, my savior." Psalm 106:21 says of the Israelites, "They forgot God, their Savior." In Isaiah 43:3 God says, "I am the Lord thy God, the Holy One of Israel, thy Savior," and verse 11 adds, "Beside me there is no savior." In His deepest, truest self God desires to save people from their sins. After learning of the child she was to bear, Mary glorified God, crying out, "My spirit hath rejoiced in God my Savior" (Luke 1:47). Expressing the deepest sentiment of any true Israelite, she glorified God by calling Him the name by which He relates to sinners—"God my Savior." God gladly receives and welcomes our prayers for the lost because He's our Savior.

2. Because of His desire (v. 4)

"Who will have all men to be saved, and to come unto the knowledge of the truth."

God is not the Savior of only those who are already saved but of all people. The Greek word translated "saved" speaks of being rescued from divine wrath and judgment. God wants all people to be saved.

a) Illustrating His desire

(1) In the Old Testament

(*a*) The book of Isaiah

In Isaiah 45:21-22 God says, "Tell ye, and bring them near; yea, let them take counsel together. Who hath declared this from ancient time? Who hath told it from that time? Have not I, the Lord? And there is no God else beside me, a just God and a Savior; there is none beside me. Look unto me, and be saved, all the ends of the earth; for I am God, and there is none else." God must make His message heard to the ends of the earth because there is no other Savior.

33

In Isaiah 49:6 God, addressing the Israelites about the work of their Messiah, says, "I will also give thee for a light to the nations, that thou mayest be my salvation unto the end of the earth." That was God's design.

In Isaiah 55:1 an invitation rings out: "Every one that thirsteth, come to the waters, and he that hath no money; come, buy and eat; yea, come, buy wine and milk without money and without price." How many people are thirsting for salvation? Everyone who doesn't have it. That is a universal call.

(b) The book of Ezekiel

In Ezekiel 18:23 the Lord says, "Have I any pleasure at all that the wicked should die? saith the Lord God, and not that he should return from his ways, and live?" In Verses 30-32, answering the questions He raised in verse 23, God says, "Repent, and turn yourselves from all your transgressions; so iniquity shall not be your ruin. Cast away from you all your transgressions, by which ye have transgressed, and make yourselves a new heart and a new spirit; for why will ye die, O house of Israel? For I have no pleasure in the death of him that dieth, saith the Lord God; wherefore, turn yourselves, and live." The death and damnation of wicked people does not please God.

In Ezekiel 33:10-11 God says to Ezekiel, "Therefore, O thou son of man, speak unto the house of Israel. Thus speak, saying, If our transgressions and our sins be upon us, and we pine away in them, how should we then live? Say unto them, As I live, saith the Lord God, I have no pleasure in the death of the wicked, but that the wicked turn from his way and live; turn ye, turn from your evil ways; for why will you die, O house of Israel?"

(2) In the New Testament

In 2 Peter 3:9 Peter says God is "not willing that any should perish, but that all should come to repentance." No theology can be biblical and teach that God is pleased with the damnation of the wicked or that He doesn't want all people to be saved. God has commanded "all men everywhere to repent" (Acts 17:30). Christ told His disciples to spread the message of salvation to the entire earth (Matt. 28:19-20). Hell itself was originally prepared for the devil and his angels, not for humans (Matt. 25:41).

b) Explaining His desire

(1) God wants everyone to be saved

Since God is Savior, He wants "all men to be saved, and to come unto the knowledge of the truth" (1 Tim. 2:4). Salvation occurs when someone comes to "the knowledge of the truth." The Greek word translated "knowledge" (*epignōsis*) speaks of a deep, complete knowledge. That word is used in 2 Timothy 2:25 to refer to the Lord's using His servant to bring people to "repentance leading to the knowledge of the truth" (NASB). Second Timothy 3:7 mentions people who have a form of godliness but no reality (v. 5), "ever learning, and never able to come to the knowledge of the truth." In Titus 1:1 Paul compares faith and knowledge (*epignōsis*), which are both elements of salvation. *Epignōsis* is used four times in the pastoral epistles and refers to true, deep knowledge that brings about salvation.

Some believers in the Ephesian church apparently believed God willed the damnation of Gentiles, and others believed God willed the damnation of those who never attained mystical knowledge. Paul confronted those deviations and affirmed that because God is by nature our Savior, He wills all people to be saved through coming to the full knowledge of saving truth in Jesus Christ.

35

(2) Not everyone will be saved

Some believe that because God wills all people to be saved, ultimately everyone will be saved. Because the Bible clearly teaches that hell exists and that many people will end up there forever (cf. Matt. 7:13-14), others conclude that God will save only those whom He wants to save, and He doesn't want to save all. They decide that "all" must actually mean "some."

The problem can be easily resolved by understanding the Greek word translated "will" in 1 Timothy 2:4 (*thelō*). There are two primary Greek words translated "will": *thelō* and *boulōmai*. *Thelō* speaks of desire springing from feeling and inclination. *Boulōmai* speaks of a precise determination. Here Paul is not saying that God has precisely determined the salvation of all people—overriding man's choice—but that God wishes it were so.

God's will of precise, sovereign predetermination moves inexorably along an unalterable track. But people constantly violate His desire, His moral will. Sin is contrary to God's will, so whenever someone sins, he violates God's will. God desires the salvation of all people, but He will not crystallize that desire into a sovereign edict, eliminating man's choice. God's moral will is subject to man's response. When God asked Israel, "Why will ye die, O house of Israel?" (Ezek. 18:31), He underscored man's choice. When someone goes to hell he does so not because of the predetermined choice of God but because of his own personal rejection of Jesus Christ.

I believe in God's sovereignty, election, and predestination, but I also believe that those who are not saved have made a choice and are responsible for it. Although I can't fully explain how those two statements harmonize, I know this: God's heart is broken because He desires that every person on earth be saved. Jesus, weeping over Jerusalem, said, "How often would I have gathered thy children together, even as a hen gathereth

36

her chickens under her wings, and ye would not" (Matthew 23:37)! We must intercede for all people because God wills them to be saved and because salvation is their highest good both now and forever.

Focusing on the Facts

1. What stifles aggressive witnessing and evangelistic praying (see p. 24)?
2. Explain the problem with evangelism in Ephesus (see p. 25).
3. What is one of the church's highest priorities (see p. 25)?
4. Why do Christians often neglect to pray for governmental leaders (see p. 25)?
5. Explain the benefit of evangelistic praying (see pp. 26-28).
6. What can happen to someone reared in a distinctly Christian environment (see pp. 26-27)?
7. If we suffer persecution and bear the resentment and animosity of our society, the reason should be that our _____ and _____ is _____, not that we are _____ and appear to be an _____ (see p. 28).
8. Define "good" in 1 Timothy 2:3. What does it explain about evangelistic praying (see p. 30)?
9. Does John 17:9 contradict the principle of evangelistic prayer? Explain (see pp. 31-32).
10. Why does God heartily accept our prayers for the lost? Explain (see p. 32).
11. What question does God ask in Ezekiel 18:23? How does He answer it (see p. 34)?
12. A theology can't be biblical if it teaches what? Support your answer with Scripture (see p. 35).
13. Define *epignōsis* (see p. 35).
14. Define *thelō* and *boulōmai*. Explain how that distinction affects the meaning of 1 Timothy 2:4 (see p. 36).

Pondering the Principles

1. Christians often misunderstand their biblical responsibilities to the government. In the face of governmental persecution or opposition, Christians are easily tempted to respond with verbal

slander or civil disobedience, especially in democratic societies, where the price of doing so isn't as high as elsewhere. How well do you understand your responsibility to your government? What are your attitudes toward those in authority? What do you usually say about them to others? Three passages capsule the New Testament's teaching about our duty to government: Matthew 22:15-22, Romans 13:1-7, and 1 Timothy 2:1-2. Read those passages carefully, noting each aspect of your responsibility and several practical ways to accomplish each. Ask God's forgiveness for any past unscriptural attitudes and behavior. To encourage yourself and to put things in perspective, read the book of Daniel over the next week and pay particular attention to God's sovereign control over earthly governments and their leaders.

2. Many passages, such as 1 Timothy 2:3, teach that God is our Savior. In Titus 3:3-8 Paul repeats the truths about our salvation and tells Titus of the importance of constantly reminding believers of God's saving work (v. 8). Read Titus 3:3-8 slowly, meditating on what you were (v. 3) and what God has done for you (vv. 4-7). When you finish reading, express your praise and thankfulness to God for His incredible grace in saving you. Begin to cultivate a deep sense of gratefulness by reflecting daily on those truths. Notice in verse 8 that Paul gives Titus a practical result of such meditation: an increased commitment to doing good.

3
Evangelistic Praying—Part 3

Outline

Review
I. The Nature of Evangelistic Praying (v. 1b)
II. The Scope of Evangelistic Praying (vv. 1c-2a)
III. The Benefit of Evangelistic Praying (v. 2b)
IV. The Reasons for Evangelistic Praying (vv. 3-7)
    A. It Is Morally Right (v. 3a)
    B. It Is God's Will (vv. 3b-4)

Lesson
    C. It Is Reflective of God's Nature (v. 5a)
        1. One God
        2. One salvation
    D. It Is Consistent with Christ's Person (v. 5b)
        1. The need for a mediator
        2. The nature of our mediator
    E. It Is Consistent with the Atonement's Purpose (v. 6)
        1. An explanation of His ransom (v. 6a)
        2. The extent of His ransom (v. 6b)
        3. The evidence of His ransom (v. 6c)
    F. It Is Consistent with Paul's Commission (v. 7)
        1. The duties of his commission (v. 7a)
            a) To be a preacher
            b) To be an apostle
        2. The defense of his commission (v. 7b)
        3. The dimensions of his commission (v. 7c)
V. The Attitude of Evangelistic Praying (v. 8)

A. Given as a Command (v. 8*a*)
B. Directed at Men (v. 8*b*)
C. Specified as Holiness (v. 8*c*)

Conclusion

Review

First Timothy 2:1-8 discusses evangelistic praying. Praying for the lost is a serious calling that the Lord has committed to us.

I. THE NATURE OF EVANGELISTIC PRAYING (v. 1*b*; see pp. 14-16, 25)

II. THE SCOPE OF EVANGELISTIC PRAYING (vv. 1*c*-2*a*; see pp. 17-20, 25)

III. THE BENEFIT OF EVANGELISTIC PRAYING (v. 2*b*; see pp. 26-30)

IV. THE REASONS FOR EVANGELISTIC PRAYING (vv. 3-7)

A. It Is Morally Right (v. 3*a*; see pp. 30-32)

Evangelistic praying is a good thing because salvation is of great benefit to anyone who receives it.

B. It Is God's Will (vv. 3*b*-4; see pp. 32-37)

Verse 3 says that such prayer is acceptable to God. In fact, the Greek text makes clear that He receives it with great delight. That's because He wants all people to have full knowledge of the saving truth of the gospel. He wants all people to be saved.

Going Against God's Desires

Some Christians find it hard to believe that God desires all people to be saved. However, no one believes that God wants people to be disobedient or unholy. On the contrary, all evangelicals would agree that God wants all people to be holy, righteous, and sinless.

Continually in Scripture He commands people to be obedient. He calls everyone on the face of the earth to give Him honor and glory. Nevertheless, all people sin, even though that is not God's desire. We shouldn't find it difficult to understand that people go to hell against God's desire.

God gives His creation the option of going against His desires. He will not ignore the volition of man. When God says He wants all people to be saved, He doesn't mean He will save them whether they want to be saved or not; He desires it but will not save them against their will. But if they refuse, He will punish them. To imagine that God is content with the damnation of anyone is absolutely contrary to His character. If that were His will, He wouldn't call all people everywhere to repent and to come to the knowledge of the truth. God desires all people to be saved, but He will not save all people because He chooses not to violate their choice.

Lesson

C. It Is Reflective of God's Nature (v. 5a)

"There is one God."

1. One God

Today it's popular to say everyone can have his own god as long as he's sincere. But 1 Timothy 2:5 doesn't say that. In 1 Corinthians 8:4 Paul says "that an idol is nothing in the world, and that there is no other God but one." If someone chooses to worship that which doesn't exist, it is his privilege to do so. But that doesn't change the fact that there's only one God. In Isaiah 44:6 God says that as clearly as it can be said: "I am the first, and I am the last, and beside me there is no God." Mark 12:29-30, quoting Deuteronomy 6:4-5, says, "Hear, O Israel: The Lord our God is one Lord; and thou shalt love the Lord thy God with all thy heart, and with all thy soul, and with all thy mind, and with all thy strength." You can love God with all you have to give because there's no other god to share your love with. That there is only one God is a central truth in the Old Testament. In fact, Deuteronomy 6:4-9 constitutes the *shema*, the

Jewish confession of faith. Although the nations surrounding Israel practiced polytheism, Israel stood for one God.

2. One salvation

Paul's point is this: there's only one God. If there were many gods, there would be various ways of salvation. Today many people insist that we recognize all the gods that people worship because of the sincerity of the worshipers. However, if we accept their gods, we acknowledge various ways of salvation. And if all the different ways of salvation are equally effective, there's no need for evangelism. Everyone has his own way, so leave him alone.

Paul says that since there is only one Savior God, He alone is the source of salvation for all people. Thus all people stand in the same ultimate relation to Him. The universality of the gospel is inextricably bound to the oneness of God. As Paul began to delineate the gospel in the book of Romans he said, "Is he the God of the Jews only? Is he not also of the Gentiles [the nations]? Yes, of the Gentiles also, seeing [He] is one God" (3:29-30). There's only one God, so everyone must come to Him for salvation. Paul's assertion that God is one justifies the universal scope of evangelism. First Corinthians 8:4 says, "There is no other God but one." Verse 6 adds, "There is but one God, the Father, of whom are all things, and we in him." If people are to be saved, they must be saved by Him. And since God desires all people to be saved, we must pray for all people. No individual or nation can be saved apart from coming to the one true God.

D. It Is Consistent with Christ's Person (v. 5*b*)

"There is . . . one mediator between God and men, the man, Christ Jesus."

A more literal translation of the Greek text is: "there is . . . one mediator between God and men, Christ Jesus Himself." There's only one mediator, so no one can say there are many ways to heaven and that any way or any

42

leader is acceptable. God has only one mediator through whom the world can be saved—Jesus Christ.

1. The need for a mediator

Job 9 introduces us to the concept of a mediator. In the middle of disaster, Job longed to communicate face to face with God. In verses 32 and 33 Job says, "He is not a man, as I am, that I should answer him, and we should come together in judgment. Neither is there any daysman between us, that might lay his hand upon us both." "Daysman" speaks of an arbiter, an umpire, or a mediator. In the middle of soul-wrenching circumstances, Job cried out, "I need someone who can lay his hand on God and on me and bring us together." That cry is answered in Christ. In 1 Timothy 2:5 "mediator" is the translation of the Greek word *mesitēs*, which speaks of someone who intervenes between two people for the purpose of restoring peace and friendship, or ratifying a covenant. Paul states with authority that Christ is the only mediator. There is no hierarchy of deities or intermediary gods (known as *aeons* to the gnostics). A man can't approach God through angels, saints, or Mary; there is only one mediator, one daysman, who can lay His hand on both God and man and bring them together—Christ Jesus, who is Himself man.

2. The nature of our mediator

Paul uses the Greek word *anthrōpos* for "man" in verse 5. We get the English word *anthropology* from it. *Anthrōpos* is a generic word for mankind, not the specific word for male (which is *anēr*). Christ was always God, but He became man—He is the perfect God-man. Therefore He can bring God and man together. Hebrews 8:6 says Christ has "obtained a more excellent ministry, by how much also he is the mediator of a better covenant, which was established upon better promises." He is a surpassing mediator. Hebrews 9:15 says, "He is the mediator of the new testament" (cf. Heb. 12:24). Christ restores peace and friendship and ratifies a covenant between God and man. He stands between an offended God and an offending sinner and mediates to bring them together.

If there's only one God, He alone can save. If there's only one mediator, He alone can bring you to that saving God. Therefore, all people must come to God through Christ to be saved. Speaking of Christ, Acts 4:12 says, "Neither is there salvation in any other; for there is no other name under heaven given among men, whereby we must be saved." Paul is telling Timothy that Christians should pray for all people because (1) God wants everyone to be saved, (2) He alone can save, and (3) Christ is the only mediator through whom they can be saved. Apart from Christ all people will be damned for eternity.

E. It Is Consistent with the Atonement's Purpose (v. 6)

"Who gave himself a ransom for all, to be testified in due time."

1. An explanation of His ransom (v. 6a)

"Who gave himself a ransom."

Christ "gave." In John 10:18 Jesus says, "No man taketh [my life] from me, but I lay it down of myself." His death was voluntary. He "gave *himself*"—not a portion of Himself, something He possessed, or something He really didn't need—He gave everything. Christ Jesus gave Himself voluntarily and completely as a ransom for all.

The Greek word here translated "ransom" is not the simple word for ransom (*lutron*), but is *antilutron* with the preposition *huper* following it. Instead of a kidnaping where a ransom is paid to free a hostage, *antilutron* speaks of a substitutionary ransom in which someone is enslaved to free another. It's like a father receiving a note about a kidnaped child, demanding that he take the place of his child. So the word implies more than the price paid for the release of a slave; it is an exchange. Christ exchanged His life for ours. He died our death, bore our sin, took our place. He gave Himself as a substitutionary payment for our sin.

44

2. The extent of His ransom (v. 6*b*)

"For all."

Christ did indeed exchange His life for ours, but the main point Paul is making is that He did it for *all*. Christ, the one mediator, died on the cross to provide a ransom for all people and to exchange Himself for the release of all sinners. Theologian William G. T. Shedd said, "There are no claims of justice not yet satisfied; there is no sin of man for which an infinite atonement has not been provided. . . . Therefore the call to 'come' is universal" (*Dogmatic Theology*, vol. 2 [Minneapolis: Klock & Klock, 1979 reprint], p. 482). Second Peter 2:1 says, "There were false prophets also among the people, even as there shall be false teachers among you, who secretly shall bring in destructive heresies, even denying the Lord that bought them, and bring upon themselves swift destruction." The Lord actually bought false teachers, heretics, and apostates. The sufficiency of the work of Jesus Christ extends to all people. But all people don't appropriate that work. Imagine that a medicine existed that was 100 percent effective at curing cancer. The effectiveness of that medicine would be unrelated to the number of people who used it. It would be capable of curing everyone but only those who used it would be healed. The same is true of the death of Christ. He made provision for everyone. We can't pray only for the superelite or the elect to be saved, because we don't know who they are. We should pray for all people because the sufficiency of Christ's work is applicable by faith to anyone. In John 6:37 Jesus says, "Him that cometh to me I will in no wise cast out." Revelation 22:17, speaking about the offer of salvation, says, "Let him that is athirst come. And whosoever will, let him take the water of life freely."

3. The evidence of His ransom (v. 6*c*)

"To be testified in due time."

That phrase translates a difficult Greek phrase. I believe the verse should be translated: "Who gave Himself a

45

ransom for all, which was the evidence at the perfect time." His ransom for all was the evidence of God's desire to save all people. The greatest single proof that God wants to save all people is the death of Christ on their behalf.

That evidence was presented "in due time" is another way of saying at just the right time. Galatians 4:4 says, "When the fullness of the time was come, God sent forth his Son." At precisely the right moment in redemptive history, the Lord Jesus came and bore the sins of the whole world. The potential for salvation is available to all people. Any theology that falls short of that attacks the character of God and the work of Christ.

F. It Is Consistent with Paul's Commission (v. 7)

"For this I am ordained a preacher, and an apostle (I speak the truth in Christ, and lie not), a teacher of the Gentiles in faith and verity."

1. The duties of his commission (v. 7a)

"For this I am ordained a preacher, and an apostle."

"For this" refers to what Paul said in verses 3-6. Because God is Savior and Christ is mediator, and because Christ died as a ransom for all, Paul was ordained a preacher and an apostle. Paul here is saying, "Why would I be doing what I am if salvation weren't for everyone?"

a) To be a preacher

The Greek word translated "preacher" (*kērussō*) refers to a herald, a proclaimer, or a public speaker. Because of the absence of modern media, if someone had an announcement to make in New Testament times, he went to the city square and made it. It was a time of open communication. People taught in the open, philosophers spoke in the open, and opinions were given in the open. Paul became an open-air preacher, a public herald proclaiming the gospel of Christ. Paul is saying that God ordained him to publicly proclaim the gospel. If that gospel is limited, it contradicts his calling.

b) To be an apostle

"Apostle" refers to someone being sent as a messenger. Paul was a messenger to cities and nations, publicly heralding the gospel of Christ. Why would God have sent him if salvation were limited?

2. The defense of his commission (v. 7*b*)

"I speak the truth in Christ, and lie not."

Paul reminded the Ephesians that they knew of his calling to extend the truth of saving grace as far as God would allow. As a herald, he spoke publicly. As an apostle, he reached all he could. Perhaps some in the Ephesian church would disagree with the strength of his conclusions here, so he reminded them he was speaking the truth.

3. The dimensions of his commission (v. 7*c*)

"A teacher of the Gentiles [lit., the nations] in faith and verity."

"In faith" could better be translated "in the faith," and "verity" means "with sincerity." Paul's content was correct, and his motives were sincere. God sent Paul to the nations of the world to publicly proclaim that Jesus is a ransom for all and to call them to salvation. How could Paul do that if it weren't true? He reminded the Ephesian believers that his ordination to go to all nations underscored the importance of their praying for all people to be saved.

A Powerful Argument for World Missions

First Timothy 2:3-7 is a powerful statement about the church's responsibility for world missions. As with Paul, God calls us to world missions because He wants all people to be saved. There's only one God and only one mediator for all mankind. That one mediator

47

died for all. And He calls us to be preachers and missionaries to reach all people. How could we justify evangelization if we believed for a moment that our message of "whosoever will" were untrue? If Christ didn't die for all, and if God doesn't will that all be saved, we shouldn't bother telling the gospel to others. But that is contrary to Scripture. This is a powerful argument for the universal proclamation of the saving gospel of Jesus Christ.

V. THE ATTITUDE OF EVANGELISTIC PRAYING (v. 8)

"I will, therefore, that men pray everywhere, lifting up holy hands, without wrath and doubting [dissension]."

Verse 9 begins with the phrase "in like manner," which denotes a change in subject. The Greek word translated "in like manner" also occurs in verses 8 and 11 of chapter 3, where the subject changes both times. But in verse 8 the subject hasn't changed. "Therefore" ties verse 8 to the preceding seven verses.

A. Given as a Command (v. 8a)

"I will."

The Greek word translated "I will" is not *thelō*, which speaks of the will of desire and was used in verse 4 to refer to God's desire for all people to be saved. Instead Paul uses *boulomai*, the will of purpose. It could be translated, "I demand," "I command," or, "I purpose that something should happen." Paul is now issuing a command.

B. Directed at Men (v. 8b)

"That men pray everywhere."

"Men" is a translation of the plural form of *anēr*, which refers to man not in the generic sense but as male in contrast to female (Gk., *gunē*). Paul selects his terms carefully. "I will that men [males] pray." In the Jewish synagogue only men were permitted to pray. Verse 8 seems to indicate that was continued in the church to the extent that leadership in public worship belonged to men. But apparently in Ephesus women were beginning to usurp the male role.

God's pattern for the church is that men lead the public worship. Paul affirms that by saying, "I demand of you that men do the praying."

The Greek phrase translated "everywhere" is literally "in every place." Paul uses it four times: here in 1 Timothy 2:8, 1 Corinthians 1:2, 2 Corinthians 2:14, and 1 Thessalonians 1:8. In all four places it refers to an official assembly of the church. Paul is saying that when the church officially gathers, men must lead in public prayer. The tense of the Greek word translated "pray" denotes habitually praying. Prayer for unsaved people is to be a common practice and should be an integral part of public worship led by men.

Women's Role in the Church

Because 1 Corinthians 11:5-15 teaches that women who pray and prophesy must have their heads covered, a demonstration of modesty and submission, someone may argue that women can pray and proclaim God's Word in the public assembly of the church. First Corinthians 11 does teach that a woman who proclaims God's truth or prays must exhibit a submissive spirit. However, compare it with 1 Corinthians 14:34, where Paul says, "Let your women keep silence in the churches." Women can pray and proclaim the Word but not in the formally established assembly of the church when it meets for official worship. First Timothy 2:11-12 confirms that by saying, "Let the woman learn in silence with all subjection. But I permit not a woman to teach, nor to usurp authority over the man, but to be in silence." When should they be silent? When the church gathers for its duly constituted worship. In chapter 3 Paul lists the qualifications for leaders of the church, and they are obviously written for men. Those are the men who are to pray when the church assembles for public worship.

A woman can proclaim the Word of God in many different settings but not in an official assembly of the church. That was not an unpopular teaching until certain segments of the church decided to endorse the women's liberation movement. But the distinction between the roles of men and women in the church shouldn't threaten any believer. In Galatians 3:28 Paul says men and women are equal spiritually before God. Besides, men also have to submit in the church. For example, a pastor is called by God to preach, and the men in the congregation are called to listen. That doesn't mean

49

pastors are elevating themselves and that every other man is a second-class citizen. The principle of authority and submission is simply a part of life. The rebellion of women against their God-appointed role reflects the unbiblical philosophy of society. But it's doubly sad when the church discovers that kind of chaos in its midst. Women can pray and teach the Word of God in a home Bible study, a fellowship group, a prayer meeting, a class situation, or wherever they don't assume authority over men.

C. Specified as Holiness (v. 8c)

"Lifting up holy hands, without wrath and doubting [dissension]."

Paul is obviously not talking about physical hands when he refers to "holy" hands, but we need an understanding of the posture of prayer if we're to get Paul's full meaning here. Our customary posture for prayer is to bow our heads and close our eyes. That's not a biblical practice but is certainly acceptable. It was customary for the Israelites to lift their hands as they prayed (cf. 1 Kings 8:22; Neh. 8:6; Ps. 63:4; 134:2; 141:2; Isa. 1:15). Paul's point is not that when someone prays, he must have his hands in the air, but that he must have holy hands. The hand symbolizes the activities of life because most of what you do involves your hands. "Holy hands" is a metaphor expressing purity of life. So the men who are to pray must have clean hands, which is to say holy lives.

"Without wrath and doubting [dissension]" refers to one's inner attitude. Church leaders are not to be characterized by anger and strife. They are to have pure and loving hearts. The Greek word here translated "holy" is not *hagios*, which is the normal word for holy; it's *hosios*, which speaks of being unpolluted and unstained by evil. Men who stand up in public worship to pray for the lost are to have pure lives and be unstained by the world.

Conclusion

The greatest model of evangelistic praying is the Lord Jesus Christ. Isaiah 53:12 says He "made intercession for the transgressors." Jesus prayed that sinners would be saved. His prayer on the cross, "Father, forgive them" (Luke 23:34) was a request for the Father to lead sinners to repentance and salvation. God answered His prayer on the Day of Pentecost, when three thousand people were saved (Acts 2:41). Within a few weeks, five thousand more were saved (Acts 4:4), and soon the church in Jerusalem may have exceeded twenty thousand people. Jesus prayed for transgressors to be forgiven, and the Father did forgive them in response to the prayer of His Son. Christ is our pattern and model.

Sixteenth-century Scottish reformer John Knox prayed the famous prayer "Give me Scotland or I die." Few times in the annals of history has one man had such a great impact on an entire nation. David Brainerd, eighteenth-century missionary to the American Indians, said he didn't care where he lived or what hardships he went through. What occupied his thoughts day and night was the salvation of souls. Eighteenth-century English evangelist George Whitefield cried out for the Lord to either give him souls for Christ or to take his own soul. Such was his passion for evangelism.

Evangelism begins in the prayer life of individuals and the church when it comes together to worship. Let us covenant in our hearts to pray personally and publicly for the lost. God will be pleased with our obedience, and the salvation of many souls will be the result.

Focusing on the Facts

1. What is the *shema* (see pp. 41-42)?
2. Explain the logical conclusion of Paul's statement that there is only one God (see p. 42).
3. Explain the significance of Romans 3:29-30 (see p. 42).
4. God has only one _____ through whom the world can be saved—_____ _____ (see p. 43).
5. Explain what a mediator does (see p. 43).
6. What is the significance of Paul's using *anthrōpos* for man in 1 Timothy 2:5 (see p. 43)?

7. What insight into the nature of the atonement does John 10:18 give (see p. 44)?
8. What does Paul mean by "ransom" in 1 Timothy 2:6? Explain (see p. 44).
9. What does the phrase "to be testified in due time" mean (1 Timothy 2:6; see pp. 45-46)?
10. Define "preacher" and "apostle." How did Paul's citing his commission bolster his argument (see pp. 46-47)?
11. How does Paul's choice of *anēr* for "man" affect the meaning of 1 Timothy 2:8 (see pp. 48-49)?
12. What is the significance of the phrase "everywhere" or "in every place" (1 Timothy 2:8; see p. 49)?
13. Explain the woman's role in the church (see pp. 49-50).
14. Describe the attitude that's to go along with evangelistic praying (see p. 50).

Pondering the Principles

1. Today there's tremendous pressure on Christians to compromise their biblically based conviction that there is only one God and, consequently, only one way of salvation. A person who believes those truths is sometimes characterized as narrow and uninformed. Have you been influenced by that pressure? Do you look charitably on different religious systems regardless of their beliefs? Are you impressed by the achievements or presence of religious leaders who worship other gods or espouse a different way of salvation? Memorize Isaiah 44:6, and meditate on its ramifications. Make a list of those you know who are involved in a false religion. Determine to pray for them once each week, and ask God for the opportunity to tell them about Christ.

2. First Timothy 2:3-7 is a mandate for personal involvement in world missions. From the missionaries your church supports, choose one as your personal project. Read that missionary's prayer letter carefully, noting his specific needs. Begin praying for his ministry immediately. Write and tell him of your intentions to help however you can. Send birthday cards and Christmas care packages to each member of the family. Ask if they miss any specialty items you could send. Try to involve your family or friends in praying for and supporting that ministry.

4
The Harvest and the Laborers

Outline

Introduction

Lesson
I. The Ministry of Christ (v. 35)
   A. Teaching (v. 35*b*)
   B. Preaching (v. 35*c*)
   C. Healing (v. 35*d*)
      1. A verification of His message
      2. A demonstration of God's tenderness
II. The Motives of Christ (vv. 36-37*a*)
   A. God's Compassion (v. 36*a*)
      1. Its source
      2. Its support
      3. Its specifics
         a) Explained
         b) Illustrated
   B. Man's Condition (v. 36*b-c*)
      1. The personification of helplessness
      2. The prey of uncaring spiritual leaders
   C. Imminent Judgment (v. 37*a*)
      1. The meaning of harvest
      2. The message of hell
III. The Method of Christ (9:37*b*–10:1)
   A. His Insight (9:37*b*)
   B. His Intercession (9:38)
   C. His Involvement (10:1)

Conclusion

Introduction

In his gospel Matthew systematically incorporated all the salient features of the kingship of Jesus Christ. In chapter 1 he began with the ancestry of the King—His genealogy. In the second chapter he presented the arrival of the King—His virgin birth and the fulfillment of Old Testament prophecies concerning Him. In chapter 3 we meet John the Baptist, the announcer of the King and witness of the approval of the King in His baptism. In the temptation Satan makes an attack on the King (chap. 4). In chapters 5-7 Matthew presents the King's affirmation of the Word of God. In chapters 8 and 9 we see the attestations of the King—the miracles that attest to His deity. Then in chapter 10 we meet the associates of the King as Christ calls the twelve and sends them out with the message of the kingdom. In Matthew 9:35–10:1 we see a transition from Christ's ministry to the multitudes to His individual discipling of the apostles. Here Matthew reveals the truth about Christ's ministry (v. 35), His motives (vv. 36-37*a*), and His method (9:37*b*–10:1).

Lesson

I. THE MINISTRY OF CHRIST (v. 35)

"Jesus went about all the cities and villages, teaching in their synagogues, and preaching the gospel of the kingdom, and healing every sickness and every disease among the people."

Basically, there were three specific elements to His ministry.

A. Teaching (v. 35*b*)

"Teaching in their synagogues."

A synagogue was a place of teaching. The Yiddish word for synagogue is *schul*, which is much like the English word *school*. The synagogue served primarily as a place where Israelites were instructed in God's Word. So when Christ went to a synagogue, He taught the meaning of Scripture —He taught the Old Testament in a didactic, expository manner. That is still God's mandate. When His people come together they must be taught the meaning of His Word.

B. Preaching (v. 35c)

"Preaching the gospel of the kingdom."

The Greek word translated "preaching" (*kērussō*) refers to making a public proclamation. Everywhere Christ went He announced that God was offering His kingdom to people, that there was a requirement for entry, and that entering into the kingdom brought eternal blessing. In a sense that was evangelism, whereas His teaching in the synagogue was edification. The people gathered in the synagogue to be taught and went out to proclaim. The church is to follow that pattern.

C. Healing (v. 35d)

"Healing every sickness and every disease among the people."

Since John said there wouldn't be enough room in the world to contain records of everything Jesus did (John 21:25), we know that the miracles in Matthew 8-9 were selected to demonstrate Christ's power in various settings but are in no way an exhaustive record of all His miracles.

1. A verification of His message

Christ's teaching was diametrically opposed to what the Jewish leaders were teaching—in many of His messages He actually confronted and attacked those leaders. Why should the people believe such messages? Why should they listen to a man from Nazareth who was not educated in the proper schools? His miracles convinced them He was of God and verified His message. The blind man Jesus healed rightly concluded that if Jesus were not of God, He could not have healed him (John 9:33). Nicodemus the Pharisee said to Christ, "No man can do these miracles that thou doest, except God be with him" (John 3:2). Jesus Himself said, "Believe me that I am in the Father, and the Father in me; or else believe me for the very works' sake" (John 14:11). They were to verify the message.

2. A demonstration of God's tenderness

Jesus performed miracles to demonstrate the tender heart of God. I believe He wanted the people to know that God was not like the Pharisees portrayed Him but was compassionate, sympathetic, tender, loving, and filled with kindness. That part of Jesus' ministry is essential in ours also. In addition to teaching the Word of God and proclaiming the good news of the kingdom, Jesus touched people where they hurt and was sympathetic, kind, and caring. The people we minister to need to see that in us. Paul said, "Though I speak with the tongues of men and of angels, and have not love, I am become as sounding bronze, or a tinkling cymbal" (1 Cor. 13:1).

The writer of Hebrews noted that Jesus can "be touched with the feeling of our infirmities" (4:15), because "though he were a Son, yet learned he obedience by the things which he suffered" (5:8). He learned suffering through His humanness. Before taking on a body, God had not personally felt physical pain or the effect of rubbing against needy people. But God dwelt among us. He touched us and was touched by us, fully identifying with our pain. The uniqueness of Christianity is that we touch people. Even though we can't do the miracles Christ did, we can show His sympathetic love.

II. THE MOTIVES OF CHRIST (vv. 36-37a)

"But when he saw the multitudes, he was moved with compassion on them, because they were faint, and were scattered abroad, as sheep having no shepherd. Then saith he unto his disciples, The harvest truly is plenteous."

A. God's Compassion (v. 36a)

"When he saw the multitudes, he was moved with compassion on them."

1. Its source

Matthew's words picture Jesus looking down from an elevated place, perhaps a hillside, at a great crowd. People were always around Him. Most came because of diseases, deformities, and hunger, but as He looked beyond their physical needs, we get a glimpse into His heart. Matthew says, "He was moved with compassion." That is the expression of an attribute of God. Jesus cared because "God is love" (1 John 4:8). The reason for Christ's teaching, preaching, and healing was that God cares about people.

2. Its support

Repeatedly the gospels record that Jesus showed compassion. Matthew 14:14 says, "Jesus went forth, and saw a great multitude, and was moved with compassion toward them." Matthew 15:32 says, "Jesus called his disciples unto him, and said, I have compassion on the multitude." In Matthew 18:27 the Lord, speaking of Himself in a parable, says, "The lord of that servant was moved with compassion, and loosed him, and forgave him the debt." Matthew 20:34 says, "Jesus had compassion on them, and touched their eyes; and immediately their eyes received sight, and they followed him." Mark 1:41 says, "Jesus, moved with compassion, put forth his hand," and healed a leper. In Mark 5:19 Jesus says to a man he has healed, "Go home to thy friends, and tell them what great things the Lord hath done for thee, and hath had compassion on thee." He demonstrated compassion because His nature is to love.

3. Its specifics

   a) Explained

The Greek word translated "compassion" (*splagchinomai*) literally means "to feel something in the gut." *Splagchna*, the noun form, is used in Acts 1:18 to refer to Judas, who after hanging himself, fell and "burst asunder in the midst, and all his bowels gushed out." It refers to the midsection and the internal organs.

When the Bible talks about the bowels of the earth, it's referring to the central portion. Matthew is telling us Jesus was experiencing gut-wrenching compassion.

The Hebrews tended to express attitudes and emotions in physiological terms and not in abstractions. They spoke of the heart as the seat of thought, action, and will. For example, Proverbs 23:7 says, "As [a man] thinketh in his heart, so is he." Proverbs 16:23 says, "The heart of the wise teacheth his mouth." Hebrews 4:12 speaks of "the thoughts and intents of the heart." Romans 10:10 says that "with the heart man believeth." In Matthew 15:18 our Lord says that all evil actions come "forth from the heart."

The Hebrews thought of the intestinal area as the seat of the emotions. When someone wanted to express deep emotional pain, he said, "I hurt in my midsection." We understand that because our midsections respond to pain. When we see a horrible accident or disaster, we feel sick to our stomachs. Fears and anxieties manifest themselves in our midsections in the form of ulcers, colitis, and indigestion because that is where emotion grips us. When God, who loves beyond human capacity, encased Himself in a human body, that body was racked by the intensity of His emotions. Matthew 8:16-17 says, "They brought unto him many that were possessed with demons; and he cast out the spirits with his word, and healed all that were sick, that it might be fulfilled which was spoken by Isaiah, the prophet, saying, He himself took our infirmities, and bore our sicknesses." That doesn't mean He contracted leprosy when He healed the leper; it means He deeply felt the pain of those He healed. It brought Him agony to see what sickness did to those He loved.

b) Illustrated

In John 11 Lazarus had died, and Jesus goes to the grave. Verse 33 says, "When Jesus, therefore, saw [Lazarus's sister Mary] weeping, and the Jews also weeping who came with her, he groaned in the spirit, and was troubled." He was deeply moved, seized by anguish. Lazarus's death alone couldn't be what caused His pain, because He knew He would raise him from the dead. Instead, I believe He felt the pain of knowing that throughout human history man would have to experience the unequaled pain of a loved one's death. He felt all the anguish and pain that the knowledge of death can bring. The Greek text tells us that Jesus literally burst into tears (v. 35). Verse 38 adds that Jesus was "again groaning in himself." That could be better translated "He shuddered." He was racked with emotion. Our Lord was sympathetic by nature because He was God, and God loves His people. Peter says that God is "not willing that any should perish" (2 Peter 3:9). He by no means enjoys the sorrow He sees in the world.

The emotions Jesus experienced reveal the heart of God. In Matthew 23:37 He says, "O Jerusalem, Jerusalem, thou that killest the prophets, and stonest them who are sent unto thee, how often would I have gathered thy children together, even as a hen gathereth her chickens under her wings, and ye would not!" Luke 19:41-42 says, "When he was come near, he beheld the city, and wept over it, saying, If thou hadst known, even thou, at least in this thy day, the things which belong unto thy peace! But now they are hidden from thine eyes." When Isaiah 53:3 says our Lord was "a man of sorrows, and acquainted with grief," it refers to sorrow and grief as only God could feel it.

Matthew uses a strong word for compassion—"He was wrenched in His midsection." Puritan Thomas Watson said we may force our Lord to punish us, but we will never have to force Him to love us. Sixteenth-century English poet Anna Letitia Barbauld wrote,

> Jesus, the friend of human kind,
>   With strong compassion moved,
> Descended, like a pitying God,
>   To save the souls He loved. . . .

59

And still for erring, guilty man,
A brother's pity flows;
And still His bleeding heart is touched
With memory of our woes.

In 1 Peter 3:8 Peter calls us to have the same kind of compassion for one another. Our motivation for ministry is our love for those who are lost.

Commentator G. Campbell Morgan wrote, "There is no reason in man that God should save; the need is born of His own compassion. No man has any claim upon God. Why, then, should men be cared for? Why should they not become the prey of the ravening wolf, having wandered from the fold? It has been said that the great work of redemption was the outcome of a passion for the righteousness and holiness of God; that Jesus must come and teach and live and suffer and die because God is righteous and holy. I do not so read the story. God could have met every demand of His righteousness and holiness by handing men over to the doom they had brought upon themselves. But deepest in the being of God, holding in its great energising might, both holiness and righteousness, is His love and compassion. . . . It is out of the love which inspired that wail of the Divine heart, that salvation has been provided" (*The Gospel According to Matthew* [New York: Revell, 1929], pp. 99-100).

B. Man's Condition (v. 36*b-c*)

"Because they were faint, and were scattered abroad, as sheep having no shepherd."

Christ moved from His nature to their need. He saw the real condition of those in the crowd before Him. Their religious facade didn't fool Him; He recognized that they were desperately in need.

1. The personification of helplessness

Matthew uses two rich words here translated "faint" and "scattered abroad." Unfortunately, those English words don't effectively communicate what Christ meant. *Eskulmenoi* is the Greek word translated "faint."

It can encompass being exhausted, battered, mangled, ripped, torn, or skinned alive. As Christ looked over that crowd, He saw they were battered and bruised. *Errimmenoi* is the Greek word translated "scattered abroad." It speaks of being thrown down, lying prostrate, totally helpless. In the Septuagint (the Greek translation of the Hebrew Old Testament) Judges 4:22 uses *errimmenos* to speak of Sisera, who lay dead with a spike driven through his temples. Those words connote mangled and devastated people who have been thrown on the ground and are lying there utterly helpless. That's how Christ saw them.

2. The prey of uncaring spiritual leaders

Continuing His assessment, the Lord compares them to sheep that have no shepherd. The scribes and the Pharisees claimed to be the shepherds of Israel, but they had allowed atrocities to happen to the sheep. Christ's words are an indictment of Israel's spiritual leaders, who didn't provide pasture for them to feed in and failed to bind their wounds. Instead, the scribes and the Pharisees had flayed and mangled the people, leaving them in a pitiful condition. That is a graphic picture of uncaring leaders who harmed the sheep more than they helped them.

In Matthew 10:6 Christ refers to the people of Israel as "the lost sheep of the house of Israel." Their leaders offered a religion that instead of lifting people's burdens, compounded them. They were more concerned with inconsequential questions about the law and their traditions than the needs of the people. In Matthew 23 Jesus indicts the Pharisees. In verse 14 he says that they devoured widows' houses. Verse 4 says, "They bind heavy burdens and grievous to be borne, and lay them on men's shoulders." Jesus accused the Pharisees of shutting people out of the kingdom (v. 13). What an indictment against those who claimed to be shepherds! The same condition exists today.

Occasionally someone will tell me that I shouldn't speak against other religious groups. But those groups are shutting people out of the kingdom of God. They mangle their followers and leave them lying prostrate and helpless. That is how our Lord perceived it. It must have been wonderful when the people heard Jesus say, "Come unto me, all ye that labor and are heavy laden, and I will give you rest. Take my yoke upon you, and learn of me; for I am meek and lowly in heart, and ye shall find rest unto your souls. For my yoke is easy, and my burden is light" (Matt. 11:28-30). The yoke of the Pharisees was deadly.

Ezekiel 34 talks about shepherds who feed themselves instead of their sheep (v. 10), who don't help wounded sheep (v. 4), and who never seek lost sheep (v. 6). Zechariah 11:16 speaks of shepherds who actually eat their own sheep! They eat so ferociously that they pull apart the bones of the feet to get every remaining morsel. In John 10 Jesus speaks of thieves and robbers who climb into the sheepfold and hired hands who are unconcerned about the safety of the sheep. Paul told the Ephesian elders to beware of "grievous wolves" who would enter the flock (Acts 20:29). The Lord Himself had previously warned that false prophets wearing sheep's clothing would come (Matt. 7:15). He didn't mean they would look like sheep. Wool—"sheep's clothing"—was the usual clothing of a shepherd. False prophets are false shepherds who devour the sheep. Jesus had compassion on those who were in desperate need of a shepherd. Someone once wrote, "Let me look on the crowd as my Savior did, till my eyes with tears grow dim. Let me view with pity the wandering sheep, and love them for the love of Him."

C. Imminent Judgment (v. 37*a*)

"Then he saith unto his disciples, The harvest truly is plenteous [filled full]."

1. The meaning of harvest

Jesus changed His metaphor from sheep to a harvest. Some people say the harvest represents lost people, the elect, or seekers after God. Isaiah 17:10-11 gives us another meaning for "harvest." It says, "Because thou hast forgotten the God of thy salvation, and hast not been mindful of the rock of thy strength, therefore shalt thou plant pleasant plants, and shalt set it with strange slips. In the day shalt thou make thy plant to grow, and in the morning shalt thou make thy seed to flourish; but the harvest shall be a heap in the day of grief and of desperate sorrow." The harvest in Isaiah 17 is judgment.

Joel 3:9-14 says, "Proclaim this among the nations, Prepare war, wake up the mighty men, let all the men of war draw near; let them come up; beat your plowshares into swords, and your pruning hooks into spears; let the weak say, I am strong. Assemble yourselves, and come, all ye nations, and gather yourselves together round about; there cause thy mighty ones to come down, O Lord. Let the nations be wakened, and come up to the Valley of Jehoshaphat; for there will I sit to judge all the nations round about. Put in the sickle; for the harvest is ripe; come, get down; for the press is full, the vats overflow; for their wickedness is great. Multitudes, multitudes in the valley of decision." I believe that when the Lord saw the multitudes, He thought of Joel's harvest— a harvest of judgment. He looked beyond their current problems to a people doomed to hell. In the parable of the wheat and the tares our Lord said, "Let both grow together until the harvest; and in the time of harvest I will say to the reapers, Gather together first the tares, and bind them in bundles to burn them, but gather the wheat into my barn" (Matt. 13:30). Verse 39 of the same chapter says, "The enemy that sowed them is the devil; the harvest is the end of the age; and the reapers are the angels."

The harvest that Christ sees is not a mission field but the final judgment, the consummation of the ages, and a time of great grief. Revelation 14:14-16, speaking of that judgment, says, "I looked and, behold, a white cloud, and upon the cloud one sat, like the Son of man, having on his head a golden crown, and in his hand a sharp sickle. And another angel came out of the temple, crying with a loud voice to him that sat on the cloud, Thrust in thy sickle, and reap; for the time is come for thee to reap; for the harvest of the earth is ripe. And he that sat on the cloud thrust in his sickle on the earth, and the earth was reaped." Jesus ministered to people not only because He loved them and because of their terrible condition but also because He could see their final end. When a believer loses that vision, he loses a major part of his motive to reach the lost. In 2 Corinthians 5:11 Paul says, "Knowing, therefore, the terror of the Lord, we persuade men."

2. The message of hell

God's vengeance will come (Rom. 12:19). The writer of Hebrews observed "it is appointed unto men once to die, but after this the judgment" (9:27). In 2 Thessalonians 1:7-9 the apostle Paul paints a vivid picture of God's judgment: "The Lord Jesus shall be revealed from heaven with his mighty angels, in flaming fire taking vengeance on them that know not God, and that obey not the gospel of our Lord Jesus Christ; who shall be punished with everlasting destruction from the presence of the Lord, and from the glory of his power." It's easy to lose a sense of the imminence and inevitability of eternal judgment.

One writer said, "There is no way to describe Hell. Nothing on earth can compare with it. No living person has any real idea of it. No madman in wildest flights of insanity ever beheld its horror. No man in delirium ever pictured a place so utterly terrible as this. No nightmare racing across a fevered mind ever produces a terror to match that of the mildest hell. No murder scene with splashed blood and oozing wound ever suggested a revulsion that could touch the border lands of hell" (cited in Paul Lee Tan's *Encyclopedia of 7,700 Illustrations* [Winona Lake, Ind.: BMH, 1979], p. 552). Knowing all its repulsive realities, our Lord was compelled to reach out to people.

III. THE METHOD OF CHRIST (9:37b–10:1)

"The laborers are few. Pray ye, therefore, the Lord of the harvest, that he will send forth laborers into his harvest. And when he had called unto him his twelve disciples, he gave them power against unclean spirits, to cast them out, and to heal all manner of sickness and all manner of disease."

A. His Insight (9:37*b*)

"The laborers are few."

We live in a lost, hell-bound world that's full of hurting people. They are trapped by false shepherds, who feed them lies that damn their souls. What should a Christian do? First he must have the insight to see the extent of the need and the lack of human resources. The Bible commands us to "watch" (Col. 4:2) and to "be sober" and "vigilant" (1 Peter 5:8). Christians have to know what's happening. The harvest is plenteous, for it includes all lost humanity, but the laborers are few. That is the problem.

B. His Intercession (9:38)

"Pray ye, therefore, the Lord of the harvest, that he will send forth laborers into his harvest."

Understanding the problem drives us to intercession. Verse 38 doesn't tell us to panic or invent a great program; it tells us to pray. It's amazing that we ask the "Lord of harvest"—the judge—to send workers into the harvest to keep people from judgment. God's holiness demands judgment; His love seeks for no one to be there. Christ saw the harvest as lost humanity moving toward judgment but He said that before that day comes, we should pray that God sends forth workers to tell others the gospel. It is interesting and significant that Jesus didn't command the disciples to pray for the lost, although that is certainly appropriate (cf. 1 Tim. 2:1-8). He told them to pray for laborers. It is possible to pray regularly for the salvation of a loved one, a neighbor, a friend, or a fellow employee and remain essentially uninvolved. But as soon as we pray for the Lord to send someone to reach them, we can't help becoming open to being that someone ourselves. We become aware of our responsibility to become involved.

C. His Involvement (10:1)

"When he had called unto him his twelve disciples, he gave them power against unclean spirits, to cast them out, and to heal all manner of sickness and all manner of disease."

Intercession leads to involvement. Christ sent the disciples out to minister (10:5). The ones who were interceding became involved. God's method is that we first understand that people are lost and there are few to reach them. Then He wants us to pray for Him to send people to reach them with the gospel, and as a result, we will become involved. If you pray for laborers long enough, eventually God will enlist you. "Send forth" in verse 38 is a translation of the Greek word *ekballō*, which means "to throw out," or "to thrust forth." That instructs us to let God send laborers. When a need confronts us, we don't panic; we pray. And as we pray, we realize that perhaps the Lord will send us, just as He did the disciples. That is God's marvelous method.

Conclusion

God has called us to teach His Word, proclaim His kingdom, and touch people's lives. Our motives in fulfilling our calling should be God's compassion, man's condition, and the coming consummation. God has asked us to have insight into the problem, to intercede on behalf of the lost by asking God to send laborers, and then to say like Isaiah, "Here am I; send me" (Isa. 6:8). One person can have an amazing impact when he gets involved in the Lord's work.

One night in the East End of London during the winter of 1869-70, a young doctor was turning out the lights of the mission where he was working. He came across a ragged boy reluctant to leave. The boy begged to be allowed to sleep there. The doctor took the homeless boy to his own room, fed him, and tried to find out his story. He learned the boy was living in a hayloft with a number of other boys. He persuaded the boy to show him where the others were. They went through narrow alleys and finally came to a shed in an old clothes market. He found eleven boys huddled together asleep in the hay with only the tattered clothes on their backs to protect them from the cold. The doctor caught a vision then and there of how he could serve his Lord. Thomas Barnardo cared for those boys and started homes for neglected children. (His story is told in *Barnardo*, by Gillian Wagner [London: Weidenfeld and Nicolson, 1979].) Dr. Barnardo ministered to tens of thousands of homeless boys and girls because he had the eyes of Christ to see into the

66

darkness and the heart of Christ to draw people into the light. May God help us to minister in such a manner.

Focusing on the Facts

1. What does Matthew systematically present about Jesus Christ (see p. 54)?
2. What purpose does Matthew 9:35–10:1 serve in the overall scheme of the book (see p. 54)?
3. Explain the nature of Christ's teaching in the synagogues (see p. 54).
4. Explain the nature of Christ's preaching (see p. 55).
5. Does the Bible record every miracle Jesus did? Explain (see p. 55).
6. Why was healing part of Christ's ministry (see pp. 55-56)?
7. What is the source of God's compassion? Explain (see p. 57).
8. Explain the significance of *splagchinomai* (see pp. 57-58).
9. What does Matthew 8:16-17 teach (see p. 58)?
10. Why does Jesus burst into tears in John 11:35 (see p. 59)?
11. Explain the significance of the Greek words translated "faint" and "scattered abroad" (see pp. 60-61).
12. What does Matthew 7:15 mean (see p. 62)?
13. What is the meaning of the harvest in Matthew 9:38? Explain (see pp. 62-63).
14. The Christian must have insight to see the _____ of the _____ and the lack of _____ _____ (see p. 65).
15. What are we to pray for according to Matthew 9:38 (see p. 65)?
16. Intercession leads to _____. Explain (see p. 66).

Pondering the Principles

1. Matthew 9:36, along with a host of other verses in the gospels, teaches that God is compassionate. That is not, however, a description of God that is peculiar to the New Testament. God's compassion is frequently an object of praise in the book of Psalms. Read Psalm 103:8-14, noting how the psalmist compares God's compassion to an earthly relationship (see v. 13).

Make a list of the ways in which God shows His compassion to you, using verses 8-14 as your guide. Take time to praise God for His compassion and for the particular ways He has shown it to you. Meditating on our Lord's compassion makes us painfully aware of our own lack of it. Ask God to begin to make His compassion evident in your life and ministry.

2. Think of a person you're praying will be saved and ask yourself this: Have you been praying biblically for him—both for his salvation *and* for someone to tell him about Christ? Stop now and ask God to send someone to tell him the gospel. Prayerfully consider if you are the one God wants to send. If so, realize that involvement in the life of an unsaved person doesn't usually merely happen; it requires thought and planning. Decide on a practical way to build a bridge of friendship between you and the one you're concerned about, such as inviting him to a family cookout or outing. After you have begun to earn his friendship and respect, seek opportunities to tell him about Christ.

Scripture Index

Topical Index

Atonement, the
  evidence of, 45-46
  explanation of, 44-45
  extent of, 45

Barbauld, Anna Letitia, compassion of Christ, 59-60
Barnardo, Dr. Thomas, ministry to neglected children, 66-67
Brainerd, David, evangelistic prayers of, 51

Church, primary objective of, 14, 20
Citizenship. *See* Government
Compassion. *See* God, compassion of

Election. *See* Predestination
Evangelism
  prayer and. *See* Prayer
  reason for world. *See*
    Missions
Evangelistic praying. *See* Prayer

God
  compassion of, 56-62, 67
  desires of. *See* Will of God
  oneness of, 41-42, 52
  sovereignty of. *See*
    Predestination
  tenderness of. *See* compassion of
  will of. *See* Will of God
Government
  involvement in, 27-30
  obedience to, 18, 26-27
  peacefulness in, 26-30
  prayer for, 17-20

resistance toward, 28-30, 37-38

Healing. *See* Jesus Christ, ministry of
Hell, description of, 64

Intercession. *See* Prayer

Jesus Christ
  advocacy of, 15-16
  atonement of. *See* Atonement
  compassion of, 56-62
  kingship of, 54
  mediation of, 42-44
  ministry of
    healing, 55-56
    preaching, 55
    teaching, 54-55
  tenderness of. *See* compassion of
Judgment, imminence of, 62-64

Knox, John, evangelistic prayer of, 51

Leadership
  characteristics of church, 50
  role of church, 48-50
  sex of church, 48-50

Man, condition of, 60-62
Martyn, Henry, on pagan worship, 20
Men, role in church, 48-50
Missions, world
  involvement in, 52, 65-66
  limited number of laborers in, 65
  prayer for, 52, 64-66

73

reason for, 47-48, 62-64
Morgan, G. Campbell, on compassion of God, 60

Persecution, causes of, 28-29
Political activism. *See* Government
Prayer
    evangelistic
        benefit of, 26-30
        biblical nature of. *See* importance of, legitimacy of
        de-emphasis of, 8, 11-12, 17-18, 31
        importance of, 8, 13-14, 24
        instinctiveness of, 8
        intensity of, 8-11, 51
        legitimacy of, 8, 11
        nature of. *See* specifics of
        qualifications for, 48-50
        reasons for, 30-37, 40-48, 62-66
        reluctance toward. *See* de-emphasis of
        scope of, 17-21, 25
        scriptural examples of, 8-11
        significance of. *See* importance of
        specifics of, 14-16, 21, 25, 68
        time and energy required for. *See* intensity of
    for the lost. *See* evangelistic

intercession, 15-16
supplication, 14-15
thanksgiving, 16
Preaching, reason for, 46-47
Predestination, God's desire for universal salvation and, 33-37, 40-41

Ransom. *See* Atonement

Salvation
    gratefulness for, 38
    oneness of, 42, 52
    predestination and. *See* Predestination
    universal, 35-37
Shedd, William G. T., on atonement, 45
Spurgeon, Charles Haddon, on evangelistic prayer, 24
Supplication. *See* Prayer

Tan, Paul Lee, description of hell, 64
Thanksgiving. *See* Prayer

Wagner, Gillian, on Dr. Barnardo, 66
Whitefield, George, evangelistic prayers of, 51
Will of God, for salvation of all, 32-37, 40-41
Women, role in church, 49-50